Sr. Joanne

Such a joy to share
this event with you.

Mac Canon Brown
2/7/14

End Hunger!

*A Poem About The Relationship
Between War and Hunger*

MacCanon Brown

❧

MacCANON BROWN PUBLICATIONS
Milwaukee, Wisconsin
2005

ACKNOWLEDGEMENTS

I am grateful for the many people of prayer and meditation I have met of many faiths and expressions of faith. They comprise my catholic, metaphysical community.

I appreciate a $300 grant from the Greater Milwaukee Foundation through the Annette J. Roberts and Joan R. Robertson Fund for World Peace, World Law and Peace Education awarded in 1990 to underwrite my costs of research for this poem.

I gratefully thank both of my sisters, Rebecca Farnbach and Jan Mitchell, for their help in preparing the original manuscript for publication. I also lovingly thank my children: Joel Brown, Ben Brown, Hannah Brown Reid and Carmella Thomas; my former husband, David Brown; and my grandchildren; for the sacrifices they make in their lives based on my path and destiny.

I appreciate the influence of my friend Julie Enslow, lifelong peace activist, on the direction of this book. Another significant presence is my former employer and friend, Doug Woodard. This book honors the Christian farm people of Iowa who were a major presence during my early years. My acknowledgements also include the uncountable homeless who have become my Milwaukee "family" in Milwaukee; as well as the network of individuals whose lives intersect with mine in their devotion to the work of the Repairers of the Breach organization. This book also honors the influence of veterans, especially Viet Nam survivors, Black and disabled vets.

It is an honor to include an illustration by my friend Stella DeVenuta, OSF, artist and spiritual director.

NOTE

I wrote this poem during the years 1987-1991. In 1992 I put it into storage indefinitely, but reclaimed it when the United States invaded Iraq. As the poem comes into its first publication, the text is very close to the original manuscript although many contemporary facts mentioned in the poem have changed.

As Stephen Vincent Benet expressed in the opening pages of *John Brown's Body,* it has also seemed unnecessary to me "to encumber this literary work with notes, bibliography and other historical apparatus."

Thanks to Iowa small press publisher Timothy Fay, my goal to publish *End Hunger!* upon the 150th anniversary of the publication of *Leaves of Grass* is fulfilled.

I invite the reader to hear the cry of hunger and to respond.

MacCanon Brown

To my Parents

ROBERT and VERLA MacCANON

END HUNGER!

Axblade and throbbing helve come crashing through
American conscience comatose frontier.
The scream of hunger sharper than horror
a scream peopled by voiceless streetcallers
camped upon curbs coughing vertabrae into grates.

They are heard like a self heard through bones.
In sepulchres of heartland hills
the reclining agrarian dead
pain to hear them
and in their granitewear skin waken
still holding cosmos flowers from seventy summer
    gardens,
dried bouquets twined upon their chests,
still remembering the hammering heart
from the terror at the tinyness of a seed,
the perilous mutuality of being its knower and
    grower
while being the seed's reason to grow
and beggar for that reason's need; even supplying
the being out of which is imagined and made
the hoe, the sickle, harrow, wheelbarrow.
The buried prairiedweller
was the body that was the work
who in that work's contortions, year by year,
became like the thrust and worried glide of plow,
like the sweat-bathed, wheezing, burdened beast,
for the sake of yield, became the seed's own How.

Sowers and reapers claybound corpses
who dwell in the pavilion of the cotyledon

take the paroxysmal quavering cry
of simulated Indias in American cities
screaming silently enough to wake the dead;
take that cry as their own
like a ewe claims a bleating lamb.

Four hundred generations of cropgrowers
answer the cry of the alienated American
from deep beneath life-giving soil.
They groan in the form of storm
in a montage of emblems of their writhing souls,
dust, orange vapor, chaff,
they wail in a wind whirling and crashing
against concrete urban premises of arrogance.

A shout from beloved rubble
of grottoes of stratified skulls,
pelvic fragments, mandibles, femora
of leathery people whose squinting eyes
saw the horizon of North America
like a flaring rim bowl, stenciled
against melting Pleistocene ice sheets,
and crossed over, shouting,
with herds of mastodon and bison.

In their deposits of dream and memory,
in their station of spirit slumber
looted by slugs and rats,
in their calcium existence buried beside dogs,
the shaman still clucks his chant into swaying smoke,

the warrior youth still sings at the coyote's
    instruction,
the squaw still holds to her heart,
then fastens to her hair,
bird effigy as token of marriage;
jars, amulets, awls within arms' reach;
bone needles, stone adzes
glazed with clairvoyance come from human grasp;
deer effigy head, beaver tooth gouge
outstay their plagued and fevered flesh.

Here is fragmentation animated into pandemonium
from the pulsar of primitiveness,
from the hawk's eye,
from the vanished people's experience with
starvation,
from the whelp-twitch moment of their instinct to
    survive.

Is it sketched on a gourd waterjug,
the woman crouched?
She has found plants growing up
where she had spilled seeds.
Her eyes are framed by her fingers held pressed
to her temples.
Cupping one's hands to drink from a waterfall
is like her mind comprehending
the connection of plant to seed.
Her blinking eyes the link between
the hunger to know and the vast unknowing.

Centuries of the pyramidal human family hear her
   gasp.

They also hear the soft, sad song
of she who rose in the morning
doubting her husband's hunt.
He is gone for a whole week;
what he brings will last two days.
He raises his hand to strike her when she complains,
but thinks of his son knurled in her protruding belly.
Her bowels are cramped from a diet of berries and
   roots.
Nearly fainting, using a stick for a hoe,
she does what no one has done before:
she plants a stand of maize, nearly a small field,
to harvest for winter, to have on hand,
even though he will be insulted and beat her,
even though he will scowl and hang his head
when he is with the other men.
The cry coming from that woman now,
crushed beneath spread-eagled skeletons,
is deeply scarred and bright
like a comet on a buckskin star chart.

Her lament against meagerness is the same
as the Inuit people of the North,
when seal and walrus are scarce, facing
their anemia, lowered resistance to cold;
same as Efe Pygmies in a dry season
coping with hunger and parasites;
same as the Mahishyas of Chakpota in West Bengal

whose infants die when food is insufficiently
   produced.

Their lament is her lament;
she, the native barefoot earth mother of American
   soil,
thin mother of American agriculture, cries out
in ancient anonymity at the atrocity
of the hungry American.

What stirring now foments in blackened blood
of buried bones under piled blankets
of vanished virgin grasslands of the plains,
as all the long-gone people of the land
pick up the cry, "End hunger!"
With the fury of clouds of grasshoppers,
storms of hailstones large as fists,
winds blinding thick with topsoil,
they'll object until they're heard.

One woman whose weeping was heard above wolves
while a Kansas snowstorm covered her house,
beneath her gravemound starts moving her lips:
"In 1860, for sixteen months,
no drop of rain; our crops dried up,
our cash was gone. Our children ate grass,
frozen potatoes, parched corn and acorns.
We lived through it and kept the land."
She tries to shout but can barely talk.

In pine wood coffins pioneer women
rouse their senses to the uproar
like to frantic prayer or a prairie fire.
Would they regard with resignation
starving conditions of street populations,
resigned as they were to the jutting ribs
of hard, lost years and howling winds
in desolate places of men's daring dreams,
silent as they were in acquiescing
to the grueling work, to their early graves?
Mute from the prospect of pangs of childbirth
being the bells' toll of each year's tomorrow,
what voice could they add if they awaken?

Pioneer women draped with pining,
penless writers of unwritten diaries
who openly spoke of soapmaking, sewing,
hauling the water, butchering hogs,
God's forgiveness, cow care and gardens,
but merely whispered, barely mentioned
sex or childbirth, menstruation,
birth control or abortion;
smiling women on iron with sedatives
never disclosing their deep depressions
or inflamed breasts or bleeding ulcers
or undiscussed torment of unusual discharge
or pleurisy or painful menses,
now speak out in powerful silence.

Heartland women gone to heaven

gone from smallpox gone from pneumonia
costly cholera costly typhoid,
theirs were the hands, theirs were the hearts:
food was their life, food was their life.
Pioneer women draped with pining
speak out now in powerful silence.

The shout and crying out will come from men
with blistered hands from digging graves
of wives and infants so swiftly,
so easily, so quietly, so indiscriminately
taken by plagues, weakened as they were
from scarcity, from damp and chill
of shack or sodhouse.
From men who grew numb from last embraces
of stiff bodies wrapped in flannel
will come a cry more like the howl
of wind ransacking unpicked cornfields
where cornstalks, cruciate with ice,
crumble and rot.
How they stare now from photographs,
unsmiling, seated in porch swings,
wearing starched white shirts,
they who followed oxen from morning till twilight
steering iron plows, their muscles and backs
on fire with pain, their sweating faces
red as cinnabar,
tall in the boy-blush sunrise of young adulthood,
in the high kick,
in the full fistful

of the dream that was land that was dream,
wide-eyed with the opening of the American
    wilderness,
buying claims and cabins, bringing brides.

They poured into the middle west
in a procession of dreamers possessed
as if a trumpet call had sounded in clear, pure tones
from a trumpeter pacing
invisibly within
a walnut grove balustrade of fieldsky,
a trumpet call at high noon
during which no leaf stirred or no bird flew,
the only activity being
the maximum photosynthesis
of conscious human will.
That there could be enough
on the level of all:
to be used by that idea,
they came.

Not asked by earth's radiant heart,
still ocher with creation's heat;
not asked by the nebula suffusion
of space breathed and touched
that is sky; not asked
by the great, moving murals
of water;
but by the all-encompassing furthermost
of a globe with all processes

springing from mutuality.

O nucleus, nucleus,
your face behind the shisham surface of the sight
is child extending empty bowl.

This egg-shaped universe's sacred flower:
a stalk of fennel
with petalled domes of astral fire for blooms.

In grasses by a river
close to nests of field sparrow and wild turkey,
pioneer children braided fennel
to wear as crown and garland.
Sons and daughters
of royalty
who were portrayed on Millet's muddy canvas
and described in Edwin Markham's poem
as "slaves of labor,"
as "monstrous things distorted and soul-quenched,
bowed with the weight of centuries . . .
dead to rapture and despair . . .
with Time's tragedy in . . . (their) aching stoop."

But times their lovemaking and laughter
filled a blue sky like oriental asterisks
from festivals of cottonwoods.
Their prayers were incessant rivers.

Their dreams' questions opened

like wings of monarch butterflies,
these folk who could hardly feed themselves
but began the attempt to feed the world.

Whatever nourished them
to be this great expense? To be
this vitality, poured out in tons
like lime into foundations,
like lime from limestone boulders
melted down massively in huge kilns;
the love-sweetened youthfulness of their bodies,
their minds trembling with meaning of coronas
and comets, all gone to ashes, melted down
into foundations of American agriculture.

What nourished them? Words of scripture;
melody of meadowlark; the gossip of newsmaking
     history;
shiny inventions: brilliance of phases
of sunrise coming up over a valley;
familiarity's softness coagulating very close
in the sight, sound and feel
of everything and everyone near,
that growth of dearness sustaining them
like a clod of living earth
clumped around a root system.

Oppressed as they were
with concatenations of work,
and shattered by bad luck and weather's brunt,

still they held on to the thought of abundance.

They spent their whole soiled lives
pressed to the juggernaut of food supply,
season after season
steeled like midwives
kneeling through quakes.
Did Pan's flute blare in those ancestor's sinews
like steam screaming from locomotives?
What force, like what could lift zeppelins,
cemented their presence
to whatever ripens or thrives?
What would have had them be
to golden ear, to mellow fruit, to fat calf,
have them so omnific,
vital as silver to daguerreotype?
For Life they did this.

For Life!—they lived and died
in plunges of wind through valleys,
by hills turbaned with sunsets,
like scenes the toddler named Manya
was even then storing in memory:
signatures of Life and death of the Polish
        countryside,
rivers and groves releasing their cycles of peace.
On her uncle's farm she clapped to see
the burst from far to near
in meeting the eyes
of his fifty thoroughbred horses outlined in sunlight,

saw Life as peace and force and radiance. Life!
Later, she and Pierre Curie
brought back from bicycling hours
armsful of sighing fieldflowers,
sighing with Life.
For Life!—the pioneers, coughing into bandanas,
birthed their lustrous hay ricks at their bodies' cost.
Also Curie would be burned
by what she found to give.
What she meant for healing
went to lethal ends,
created mass, steep graves.

So Life is creative, Einstein had mused
before he walked the very same grid
of connected cobblestones as the Curies,
before he gazed out a window near their windows
and would eventually choose to remove
the smock of nuclear specialist,
having no hand in what would happen
to Hiroshima and Nagasaki.
In an atlas of human anatomy
he found "more formidable complexity"
than in all solid or fluid earth.
Toward the walker on the land more awe
than for the land walked upon.
This "more creative individuality,"
he said, "is creativity."
The man with the hoe, the toiler
through "whose dread shape the suffering ages look,"

embodies the knowing
which is Life becoming
the being of
its livingness.

The French peasant gleaning a field's final sheaves,
Cather's Shimerda lighting his lantern,
Ferber's cabbage growers loading up their wagons,
pioneers pouring their milliards
of drops of sweat into days.
For Life! ‑ ‑

We would have them sleep in the even breath
of infinite rest soft as slumbering embrace.
This death: warm, warm as woodheat, deep
as lilac paths in moonlight.
We would have them sleep
relieved of pain, all worries calmed,
assured their lives were more than thistleseed.
In chambers still as autumn bronze
reflecting northern lights
we would have them sleep.

But they cannot rest, so cramped in pain
to hear the cry of hunger in the land.
In shocked integrity, in torment they complain
at why those who are hungry are not fed,
and weep like broken monuments,
and lie in anxious wakefulness
when we would have them sleep.

Their cries filter through leadened films
of knowing nonexistence;
their hoarse post-mortem cries
cross margins of two centuries
like ink bleeding through months.

In rubble left from World War I,
Eastern Europe found no food.
Where Paderewski's music still echoed,
eagles white as bread circled, soared
like Quaker hearts in search of inner peace.
Crops destroyed by war.
No seeds for a new crop.
Wind bearing tunes of the pianist Paderewski
helped sparks rise from factories chimneys' smoke
into sky wide as Quaker charity.
The daily bread of Polish people seven ounces each.
Herbert Hoover, orphaned at ten,
head of the American Relief Administration,
called for relief operations
beginning with the children.
Armenia with no bread anywhere,
or in Syria: not a dog, cat or camel to be found.
In the rural America of Hoover's Quaker origins,
chaff from threshing machines
was falling on hung out wash,
blowing into eyes of farm women,
eyes where tears of sympathy were flowing springs;
buxom women who prayed for the hungry
while they built fires under kettles at dawn

to wash hills of laundry; then cooked huge meals
for chaffy threshing crews, giving the nod
for a blessing to be said, the table grace of thanks.
Women who prayed with chapped, red hands,
who moved as surely to their tasks
as Chopin's humanitarian sister Ludwika
lifting his three-year-old hands to the keys.
Where 10,000 Europeans would die in one week,
people were turning to cannibalism.
Women stripped flesh from dead horses.
Near Hoover's Quaker family home,
home of his uncle, who worked among Indians;
of his great uncle, minister to prisoners;
of his guardian, Laurie Tatum,
who helped move slaves to freedom;
near Hoover's birthplace,
young Grant Wood, son of a Quaker,
was thinking about shocks of corn:
how tall, how embroidered with intermeshed fiber,
how golden, how gauzy,
how totemic, how timeless.
Millions of children. Tons of foodstuffs
by ship, by rail, by camel train.
Food for ten million people a day.
Long, leaning lines of relief canteens.
Beyond hunger, the longing for peace,
pale lily in scraggly forests of nationalism;
pale as the face of Chopin's sister Emily
who died, a budding poet, at age fourteen.
To Quakers, the world is a dwelling of the spirit

in which the means of its redemption are present.
"No government rests securely
while its population starves" ⸌⸌
words of Herbert Hoover.
Flour, beans, peas, rice, milk.
Lines of naked children being weighed, measured
to determine malnutrition.
Threshing crews getting up from their tables,
hauling water to start the whooping engines,
situating belts on pulleys;
brawny men brushing chaff from their eyes,
eyes used to becoming instantly moist with kindness.
These farmers moved as surely to their tasks
as Grant Wood's paintbrush to his mural;
their hands, arms, backs
forking, pitching, hauling in cooperative rhythm
food to save one third of Europe.

People in Moscow fainted in streets.
One half of the Ukraine's population would starve.
Lenin said to his Tenth Congress,
"*If* there is a harvest . . . "
Colonel Haskell to Herbert Hoover:
"As a Christian nation
we must make a greater effort
to prevent this tragedy."
The Polish foreign minister wrote:
"Although Poland has . . . been under the oppression
of the Russian yoke, yet the Polish Nation
feels the ill treatment to which they were subjected

was caused by the Russian government
rather than the Russian people.
It is the sincere desire of the Polish Nation
to lend a hand of friendship and help
to the suffering Russian masses."
Five hundred forty thousand tons of food in two
    years.
Three thousand relief kitchens in towns, villages.
Herbert Hoover said:
"The sole object of relief should be humanity.
It should have no other political objective or aim
than the maintenance of life and order."

Corn meal and seed corn from Iowa.
Dried milk from Wisconsin.
Help came to those people's needs
as surely as Emily Chopin's poetic vision
became the composer's melodies:
the Vistula, flowing with tears over war after war,
the Carpathian's crystal lattices of waterfalls
like promptings of truth to which Quakers move.
Kamenev, speaking for survivors near the Volga:
"The wall that separates us from America
will crumble sooner than will be the case
in respect to other countries."
Outpourings of gratitude to America
expressed as surely as Chopin's Etude in E, Opus 10
flowing from Paderewski's hands.
Documents glowing with inner light:
albums of thousands of school children,

scrolls of thousands of autographs
sent to Herbert Hoover thanking America.

Long since have those same burly farm folk
shifted their suasion to roses,
to roses.

For beyond the need for bread,
past hankerings for peace,
the love of beauty aches,
for beauty.

Their children who put coins in their eyes, tarnished
    coins
with presidents' faces,
removed those coins and found their eyelids
soft as dewy petals.
As petals.

Their spent bodies are buried
downhill from soldiers,
from soldiers.

In graves beside clay-tiled cornfields,
their prayers for the unfed poor become shouts,
become shouts.

Their voices echo through mazes of orange vowels
into the earth's sighing bosom,
her bosom.

Saying, "We would not have our bodies be immortal.
For our words to endure we do not ask.
Not ask."

"All we want is for our work to be all done.
This would be our thanks and our glory,
our glory."

"For every human being to have food
would be all we need of thanks and glory,
and glory."

Links they are, links between
their time and time to come,
those who made the crossing to mechanized farming,
who worked in innocent consecration
even when chelate with industrialization.
To the abominable snowmen we bring their
    silhouettes
To theoreticians we bring their hand's shadows.
To abominable snowmen chewing their tongues
    abominably
at symposiums of social scientists
wondering what will become. To abominable
    snowmen
who blink and rub their static abominable fur
in legislative bodies and congressional committees
purring with power mixed with valium or cocaine,
wondering what will become.
Through abominations of chaincurtains of stale
    smoke

where aplomb abominable snowmen sit
abominating in swivel chairs
at conference tables of multinational corporations
supporting production of bombs.
Tell them the human body is the unified field
designed to overcome the suffering of the world.
That we are streamlined to bring peace and nutrition,
to develop human machinery
to cultivate potential.
Let them view the embalmed bodies of rural
    ancestors,
let them worship their lime anatomies,
let them lift their little ones to look in their caskets
letting them squirm to bend from arms around their
    girth,
hearing them beg to touch the land of farmers' cheeks,
to see the eternal grandparents of all of us.
We are linked to those rural ancestors by the need
to feed the overpopulated world. Connected
as if sharing a common placenta: the universe,
tense to recreate its creativity
in the imagination of unity.
Links between their time and time to come,
they show how systems of sharing begin with land
    and hands.
Tell genetic engineers and sculptors,
anthropologists and choreographers,
for ideal future human beings
we would suppose Johnny and Johanna Appleseeds,
earth-tending, but not possessing earth;

God-seeking, but not crusading a God;
belonging to everyone, but self-sufficient alone;
loving not so much for love the people on their way,
but for leaving in their tracks such green, green
sprigs of tranquility for Spring, Spring
to mark their reverent vagrancy.
Not to worship or let the dream come true
imagined in fiction of Stranislaw Lem:
an "intellectronic" Creation named "Setaur"
(Self programming Electronic Ternary Automaton
    Racemic).

Stands seven feet high, moves fifty kilometers an
    hour.
Teflon friction joint surfaces. Impenetrable armor.
Only a bulge for a head between shoulders.
Where its heart would be is a violet laser,
a 45,000 kilowatt middle eye
between two photoelectric eyes
made to instantly fire at whatever lies
centered in the field of vision
Juxtapose Setaur with figures of farm folk,
quiet messiahs of the malnourished.
How similar is Setaur's cry in combat
to the scream of every starving soul on earth.

How sweet the thanks of the grateful survivor.
How contour the emotion of the giver
like a wing forming in a silken case.
Not as "haves" among "have-nots"

would we offer the food. And for
more reason than for all to have some;
more motive than this. To become
conductors of what is so beyond us
we cannot know but vaguely recognize,
an inner harmonic nature dyed in daylight
we faintly claim as our matrix
like test tube babies who hear strains of Beethoven:
a core magnificence
like a prisoner in free fall paralysis of sleep
realizes before the Elysian wet dream.

Oh, pure love of peace!
Peace profound with resurrection
belonging to everyone
beginning with the refugee
who has survived one war after another;
who carries scars from the wounds of battle,
and from torture endured in imprisonment;
who knows the betrayal of governments like blows
    to a skull,
and grew deaf from the vocabulary of degradation;
with body misshapen from being often without food,
and by being beaten and broken;
humiliated from living in poverty and exile;
who has had every dignity taken away
and in replacement been given ashes and rags;
the refugee, fleeing another burning village,
stumbles in the twilight on this lily,
this wisdom of the omnipotent human spirit

which is the love of peace, pure, calm,
earned, achieved by those who have been ultimately
    wounded
and offered to the world in their transcendence.
All actions out of altruistic thought
arise from here.
Plane of life-giving harmlessness.
Universal dynamic to transact, to manifest
like in lives codified to crop growing.

Faces of farmers in phantom form
emaciated faces evanescing.
Stonebroke farmers under breadcrust gravestones
in graveyards staked with wrought iron gaps
and bars blunt as headlines bruised from crashing.
Faces of farmers long forgotten
brood from horizons figured with breadlines.
Vanished in memory, bleared with vagueness,
now they face us, eyes glassed with fear,
sensing despair in dark repetition
of dearth they knew in the Great Depression.
Faces not voices fervently speak
for those who forage for food in garbage.
Conjured by the crisis of grocery cart chattels,
their faces appear in apprehension.
Like writing on walls, their faces warn.
Anonymous faces float into mind,
camera stills of a stethoscope:
scored with smile lines, her face gone stern,
eyes shaded by brim of a calico bonnet,

a worn old woman worriedly watches
her shrugging men return from market:
a bushel of corn bringing a dime;
each pound of fat cattle, a puny three cents;
one and a half for a pound of hog.
Six tenant farmers with no farms
line up to pose, their faces, long;
wearing wrinkled overalls, sweat-ovalled hats;
two standing straight, strong arms, crossed;
one, with hands ensconced in empty pockets;
one, more sunburned, hands behind back;
two, twisting twigs; all, tense-faced.
Six tenant farmers with no farms
when personal income dropped fifty percent
in twenty-nine, when times were hard.
When farm foreclosures were five hundred per
    county,
faces of men reading fine print
in dim lamp light of a full dormitory
for homeless men, are hunched over words
describing riots, milk truck dumpings,
public outrage over burning of orange groves,
and slaughter of pigs while so many starve;
surplus products, depressed prices,
floundering banks, failing strikes.
Hunch-backed farmers over fifty
in a haven for homeless men,
sit so quietly on quilt-covered cots,
calm faces speaking catastrophe.

Hired hand Homer Sharer,
with wife, and family of five children,
in scuffed shoes, patched clothing,
unemployed and unable
to pay interest, insurance,
taxes, doctor, rent or dentist.
Relief sustains these staring seven.
The biggest boy's face is averted, frowning.
His peaked brother with unparted hair
backs up to the wall next to the window
tacked with a curtain of torn oilcloth.
His pretty little sister sits in the shadow
of the exhausted father embracing a baby
and the tired mother holding a toddler.
Faces of the family of farmer Homer Sharer
look down or away from the camera lens
or hungrily into the face of Homer,
but their faces speak directly of facing hunger.
Three dusty men determinedly wait
with tightly pursed lips by a telephone pole,
sitting and squatting, scratching the dirt,
in vigil for vital relief checks,
faces shadowed by hatbrims and shame.
In a mended jacket, another man
keeps his watch, waiting and scowling,
slouched by a window silhouetting his shadow,
half-standing now, with one knee bent
like a perching bird with a broken leg;
in a line of men looking in that window,
waiting in line, looking at their shadows,

dependently waiting for the doling
of relief money doled out monthly.
The expressions blink of extinction's brink.
The silence of their pictures makes deafening speech:
the dispossessed farmer squatting on dirtclods;
the bearded, hunched man shivering in a breadline,
a tin cup between his clasped hands and his heart;
America knew hunger like the back of his hand.
The brown-eyed child of Ed Boltinger
alone confronts the clicking camera
with frowning face and furrowed brow.
She stands beside the simple shack
of her family about to lose their farm;
no saving left for buying seed;
loans, denied; debts, too deep;
breeding stock, sold; machinery, broken.
Her soiled cotton dress covered with daisies
has a tear across her heart.
For sleeves and leggings, feedsacks serve.

No case of eggs even exists
to sell to purchase a pair of shoes.
She's hungry again in a house without food
on submarginal land in a spring without rain.
Three are tenting under a tree.
The bewildered woman breastfeeds her son.
Close to the lens, leaning on his hand,
on a ragged blanket on a bench,
her husband looks into hollow hours
of prolonged waiting for a stretch of work

in California cotton fields
far from the land they left behind.
Their abandoned farm of empty fields,
sorry with drought, where dust clouds rolled
like dirty pots, stands desolate.
The bleary-eyed young man looks back:
vacant buildings, barbed wire fences,
fields plowed up to the farmhouse door
by the tractor and plow he couldn't pay off.
Displaced farmers beaten by drought,
moneyless, malnourished, with mouths to feed,
pushed to desperation by the Depression,
six thousand a month moved to California
to work in fields as migrant farmers.
A couple enroute in a sagging car
have stalled in a ditch, are stranded there.
She leans back for his face to show,
at the steering wheel, his terrible why.
The photo shows her collar of fur
hiding her tears; seams of her hose,
lines of her forehead, hands in her lap.
She leans far back so his laid bare soul
can be the focus of the finding lens
with her body and face the living frame.
Will they give up or will they get out,
stand straight as dying trees surrounded by dunes,
to wave down cars with windmill-motion arms,
swatting at defeat like steel blades chopping dust?
Will they join the refugees further down the road,
among clotheslines and chimneys of squatter camp tents

by a tollgate of fenders, furniture and tubs?
Just to pick peas for a cent a pound,
they'll restlessly sleep all night in the row
to hold their place to pick the field.
A photo shows the forearms browned,
flapping rags of faded denim,
hardened hands that hold a hoe,
the weathered torso, tattered clothes
of one more faceless man with hoe.

Six follow behind him, fumbling lettuce leaves
in straw hats and bonnets, bending their backs.
Like an eternity, lettuce rows are endless
and the cracked soil in such connection
is sloped like a grave. They just go on,
close to fainting, past the crouched photographer.
They go on to die, the Great Depression's dregs,
but their personhoods still poignantly speak
from visual laments of their lost lands and livelihoods,
from eloquent pictures of their bare existence
when California's tableau was tiled with their backs.
Their lives eroded into the earth
from self-willed farmer unto field worker,
then unto sleep in root-meshed sludge
among the starved, among the slaughtered;
sealed lifetimes cemented to soil;
the land's own, like offspring of mother,
dovetailed into her shoulders like ducktailed children
whimpering, clinging to their worried earth mother.

Sitting in tentshade, she nurses one to sleep.
Two photo-shy children hide their faces
by snuggling into her strong body.
Wedged together, they wait for food.
The older ones are snaring wild birds
so they all can last a little longer,
she and her seven, through another season.
The pea crop is frozen, no work can be found.
Her car tires are gone; they cannot leave camp.
Her skin is not soft; her face is strained.
She pulls her cheek and props herself,
endangered migrant mother earth.
She squints beyond squatter's camp bounds
with a mother's seeing which is more a knowing,
with a similar eye as mother earth's
x-raying soul watching examino;
same seeing/believing as granule breath,
as planet tug, as ocean tide.

But this woman's gaze is glazed with doubt.
How can we live? Will our lives end?
How can we eat? What will we do?
Where will food come from? Where will we find
    some?
Where is there enough for them all to eat?
Her queries the same as mother earth's question:
where will we find sufficient food?
The question is frozen on her face
in a photo lasting beyond her life.
Same numb, forsaken seeing knowing

of those hurting, helpless, hungry, homeless
women with children while we live.

In the land of the paradox of poverty amidst plenty,
a high hill overlooks stubble fields.
On this hill and burial mound,
silence is broken by wind gusts moving
like wild herds of peccary.
By other stones, large monoliths stand:
likenesses of Pliocene forest hogs' skulls,
whose tusks do not curl; whose eyepits funnel dust,
each granule layered with skins of rampant rivers.
To this sacred bracken may come
one who is purified by shaman invocation.
When wind becomes like a litany,
then the soul of the natural world will listen,
if this question is asked from the summit,
called out from among the monoliths:
"Why do some have so little while others have so
    much?"
The soul of the natural world will answer
in a quieted rage like a smoldering fire, whispering,
"Because there are hogs and swine and pigs."

When the answer is given,
onto the scene will rush a herd of hogs
in every color of coat: white, tortoise-shell,
black, spotted, red.
Their squeals will be extreme like elephants
    trumpeting.

Their ears will be flared back on their massive heads.
Their leering eyes will glint with languor and
    aggression
while they scour the territory for food.
Tremors will move through their ribs and muscles.
Dark bristles on their stocky bodies
will stand straight up.
Whatever can be eaten will be found by them
and devoured by them.
It will be masticated by the forty-four teeth
in each hog's mouth, swallowed by the massive
    tongue,
carried by esophagus to stomach.
Every leaf, every stem in sight, they will consume,
even if they have had their fill,
even if they are full enough to vomit,
they will gobble up everything edible they see.
If there is a kernel of grain covered with earth,
in their rooting with their snouts,
one of them will find it and devour it.
Whatever is in their path will go into their mouths
and be chewed and consumed: roots and bulbs,
vines or stalks, berries and seeds;
until the landscape is devoid
of plant or shrub, fiber or flesh.
The hogs will forage till nothing is left but wasteland,
then they will move on, loudly squealing,
filling their mouths and stomachs as they go,
leaving their hoofprints behind
on the earth, a slimy, spreading spongeface.

Then will come the swine,
a herd of swine numbering hundreds,
all of them grunting and barking,
rooting up the ground with slobbery snouts,
or sniffing each other's faces and undersides.
In the dirt cloud stirred up by their hooves,
they will blindly move, sometimes colliding,
lunging shoulder against shoulder,
slashing at each other's heads with their canine teeth,
pawing the ground, chasing biting tails.
In the fighting, some of them will lose their balance
and will fall, rolling onto their backs, and lie there,
chomping, their jaws exuding foamy white saliva.
On their backs, each will lie there, frothing,
like a pig positioned for dissection
on a table in the School of Salerium
during the time of the crusades,
where, beginning with the throat incision,
the ancient anatomists, waking from the Dark Ages,
credible to how pigs resemble humans internally,
moved through their chests and abdomens,
organ by organ, then uteruses and brains.
They ended up again with the heart,
with the comment expressed in the text by Richard
    Angelicus,
"It is said all moral virtues are located in the heart."
These swine will rise to their feet, staggering,
shaking themselves, going for each other's throats,
stampeding again, trampling everything in their path,
snarling, attacking each other as they go.

Finally will come the parade of pigs,
wearing tuxedos and riding in convertibles,
who speak as humans speak, but stammering.
They are able to sing Yankee Doodle into
    microphones
for audiences of whole and broken soldiers,
and say to win the war, and they wave flags, and
    march.
Their lives last as long as Disney patriotic cartoons.
Their lives end in harnesses and racks
of ventilated radiochemical fume hoods,
where men wearing goggles and laboratory uniforms
feed them and test them for long-term effects
of very high levels of radiation.
If the wailing and crying and wanting whining of the
If the sobbing and the scared shrieking of the
If the heartwrenched
If
If
If the rising, falling pain-dulled flood of tears
If the cursing scratched into faces of the
If the moaning ending in weakened pleading of the
If the bawling that fractures into whimpers
If the weeping weeping weeping
If the
of the

War is the bloody-eyed agent of hunger.
Its fleet of winged weapons,
like blue metallic blowflies,

begin as clammy larvae
living in the carrion
of starvation's victims,
or thriving in the open sores
of the hungry and the poor.

From its crimson couch, each larva dreams
of a fireblast equal to a million Hiroshimas;
cities, forests and grasslands gone
to a cupreous smear of blaze;
with smoke of burning gas and oil wells
like cobras swaying in sky.
Here is the dream of the gluttonous grub,
smacking and chewing and gulping:
towering red cinder-filled mushrooms
numbering thousands, grander in scale
than the first one tried in forty-five,
when Oppenheimer was moved to quote from the
    Vedas.
When that lion-maned column of fury
rose on that brindled horizon of desert,
leaping from bonewhite chalkboard equations,
from skull-silent papier-mache lab models,
came to him words from the Bhagavad-Gita:
"I am become death, the shatterer of worlds."

Little larvae of nuclear warheads
snuggled into suppurating sores of the poor
dream huge cloud shapes as they slurp and drool,
clouds which are to the sacred DNA

like tarpits were to dinosaurs;
clouds with alpha and beta particles for spindrift;
clouds in which the divine DNA flounders, choking,
and fails within those missile larvae's dreams,
while those grubs lick their lips and gnaw
through prime resources of the world.

In the Destroyer's dreams
the DNA prays in the face of death,
the DNA prays in the dark of cloud.
(Cloud megaton plutonium 239 pagoda flash
    blindness)
Agnus Dei, Qui tollis peccata mundi, miserere nobis.
(Cloud neutrons Iodine 131 tea ceremony leukemia
    ozone)
Deus, Qui humanae substantiae dignitatem
mirbiliter condidsti.)
(Cloud detonation lotus hemorrhage shock was
    Cesium 137)
Libera nos, quesumus, Domine, ab omnibus malis,
præteritis, præsentibus, et futuris.
(Cloud eardrum rupture Carbon 14 radiation
    sickness kimono)
Oremus.
(Cloud thermal pulse emperor tritium cataract burns
    cancers)
De munere temporal; fiat nobis remedium
    sempiternum.
(Cloud ricebowl strontium 90 7000 Centigrade
    sterility)

Adveniat regnumtuum.
(Cloud ground burst hypothyroidism funeral pyre
    dust)
Per omnia saecula saeculorum.

Farm people will see it from their fields,
the obsession of doom when it mushrooms
from powercrazed minds of munitions maggots.
They will see it through their hands from afar
holding their hands up for shades.
They'll come in from their fields of soft, turned earth,
having seen the blast through fingertips and palmlines
as through etched glass tinted salmon, mauve.
The farm people will head north on foot en masse
and will dwindle in number as they die, then, vanish,
leaving an inscription charcoaled on a concrete slab:
    "Today the afternoon sun tried again
    to open the pore of tomorrow. Bulbs ticked
    in the ground like mines. Anniversaries
    coughed up from field nests as we
    stumbled over them. Then the sunset
    shimmered like a placenta
    drawing the last traces
    of childness out of us
    to fly into the sun
    much like pain
    toward a clove. We stood
        tapered on our bones
        and felt the flush
        of wonder leaving us

to become fuel. Later,
when the ashes fell,
we carted them to the field,
spread and groomed them with our feet
in the dark. Resting then, lovers spoke
in tremors for gestures, saying,
Face, you are family, wing, breast.
Widows made their usual gibbon search
through scalps for combs, ticks, prayers.
The weak rocked the strong all night.
Symtoms of dawn were lobed blue moths
which toured our bodies for clues
about where we were from and going.
The seeing of them and the frisk
harped our memories. We spoke in psalms
to the children, made poultices of leaves
and tears for them, and filled our hands with loam.
We sang. The near-blind received second sight.
Tender kisses of oral history were told
to the calligraphy of cheeks, so softly,
before the white peonies were passed.
We glowed with how we had ever loved.
We heard the roar, and sang:
Face, I see you with the torch of me,
Let me melt you into the coin of us."

Then from those vanished agrarian dead: no cry.
Silence. Gargoyle stone mouth silence.
Silence. Sleeping Pompeii silence,
like from Pompeiians sealed in volcanic dust,

their bodies calcined for centuries,
their heads lifted to the gods,
their mouths open from shrieking
under the hail of pumice fragments,
then the sea of ashes.
A survivor told an uncle in a letter
a cloud formation shot up over Vesuvius
"resembling a pine tree — a tall trunk
which spread at the top into branches."
impregnated with cinders,
bursting with vapor,
with a train of fire.
Fire fell, then ashes covered everything.
This silence of farm people fleeing the bomb,
same suffocation, same silence,
total silence from mouths frozen open forever.

Their deaths will also be
deaths from starvation.
Their souls will join souls
of trees and honeybees,
panatrophied, pale, lamenting;
souls of Durum wheat plants,
souls of butterflies and plankton:
a myriad of God-cameos forced into extinction.
Their souls will linger, convulsing and fainting,
ambivalent to leave.
Thousand hazarded souls of a forest,
souls of earthworm, of fieldmouse, of stallion,
all waiting for the weakened, bleeding All-Soul

to gather solemnly into its Self
the cumulative error and crime of human vengeance,
then by its pure knowingness to make shroud
and seal colossal sorrow like a book.

War is the gold-toothed slaughterer.
War is the loudly-belching confiscator of means.
War is the one-armed monger of hunger,
who wipes his nose on his sleeve
as he jingles cash
which would otherwise be spent
to relieve the suffering of the poor.
War crows about each mealsite ticket holder
knowing money is flowing into the Pentagon
instead of being poured into that life.
In countries imitating the deluxe standards
of American military prowess,
the burden of enormous debts from buying arms
falls extortionally upon the people.

Many of them lose their land, their home,
then starve while War polishes his boots.
If in their desperation they revolt, demanding food,
hoards of soldiers with teargas will overwhelm them,
brutalizing them with riot control tackle from the
	U.S.,
their survival twice squelched for War's sake.
The policeman firing the teargas canister,
his face livid with terror, speaks what fear
triggers lightning in his spine:

"If these rioting peasants
overthrow this regime,
my family and I
will starve in the streets."
Cigarette-puffing foremen of aerospace plants
know similar fears. From their padded roosts
over coops of women shackled in rubber gloves,
they are terrified that Peace might have its day
and do a fateful turnabout on them:
as arms race costs multiplied the destitute like fleas,
a cooperative laying down of arms in sweet
    de-escalation
could plunge arms manufacturers' lives,
they fear, into necessitousness.
So they make of the peace demonstrator a target
to hate, to degrade, to arrest.
What body to place between the hunger-crazed
    peasant
raging against his oppressor,
and the policeman clubbing and kicking him?
What body suppliant, motivated by pacifism,
ricocheting all the negative forces off of him?
What body to place between the jailed demonstrator
sickened with despair, grown bitter in his youth,
and the Big Guns seething with intolerance;
whose body to eclipse the furor?
Whose body, what human being, what life,
what neutral friend, referee?
To be between enemy and enemy
as an interlocker, coaxing like Jacques Bouillault

getting hen to snuggle on the fox's head.
If the spirit of dead Norman Thomas could see,
if the spirit of dead Norman Thomas could speak,
he would stand jauntily on his arthritic legs,
with his face bright and voice quavering, saying:
" . . . the peace and happiness of the world
requires a sense of brotherhood
for all the sons and daughters of earth . . .
its emphasis on
a common abhorrence
of cruelty, oppression
and everything that would reduce human life
to the status of a commodity
and man himself to the level of a thing."
Norman Thomas saw human history
as a long struggle against scarcity.
His eyes were blinded by teargas bombs,
eyes which flooded with feelings and failed with age.
But he was not blind to the blight of misery,
having seen up close the grim conditions
of rural poor distraught with pellagra,
unable to read and wearing rags.
He spoke for the farmers to F.D.R.
criticizing the controversial
Agricultural Adjustment Act.
To reduce productivity to drive up prices
Thomas called "subsidizing scarcity,"
and helped to found a farmers' union,
kind of a hornets' nest to the Ku Klux Klan.
The farmers rallied, ripe for riots,

many fearing foreclosures and evictions,
many wearing welts from floggings,
bruises from beatings,
sores from landlords' gunshot snipings.
Tractors cost then three times their value.
People were paid to plow cotton under.
People were paid to plant less wheat.
Six million pigs were methodically slaughtered.
The days were dark with oppressive debts.
When farmers were accepted by American Labor,
they chanted, "Establish justice . . . create plenty;"
"abolish tenancy . . . destroy poverty."
Thomas called for a cooperative commonwealth
for Native American and Black tenant farmers,
and White and Mexican tenant farmers.
They chanted, "Land to the landless,"
"Power to the disinherited,"
and mingled into one heap
fistfuls of soils from rural states
while saying, "The land
is the common heritage
of the people."
"They are virtual slaves . . . " said Norman Thomas.

Does Thomas see, as he lies buried?
Does he hear the cry of hunger?

He hears the starved child crying in the womb.
He hears the unborn poorest of the poor.
He hears the fetus just from ovum grown

who, as the glucose is exchanged,
holds on, though her placenta is quite small.
She grows, in membrane wrapped. She slowly grows,
afloat in amnion. These are less cells
to form the cerebellum of her brain,
and for the cerebral cortex, less neurons.
Her mother's protein is in short supply.
The braided cord sustaining her till birth
delivers less nutrition than she needs.
Her skull is small. Her weight at birth is low.
She's premature, born into midwife's hands.
She'll be mothered very close and fed by breast,
but when she's weaned, she is then pushed away
and forced to live with other relatives.
She's slapped for how she whines or cries or begs.
To eat, she has to fight for her own food,
and usually is given cornmeal gruel.
She withdraws and whines, and no one pays much
    mind.
In the crowded, dim lit house, she loses weight.
She's supervised by sibs age three and four.
Her potbelly and swelling are ignored,
her diarrhea worsens, hair falls out.
She catches an infection and is "starved"
to "purify" her body against disease.
She whines, her skin has scabies, her gums bleed,
her muscles waste away. Her growth's impaired.
Anemia and apathy take hold.
She whines, and is ignored by everyone;
she whines, and what she feels, she's taught to block,

to repress inquiry, emotions, needs;
she learns never to ask, and not expect;
she learns not to look forward to rewards
and that there's no way out of poverty.
She's from a pocket of the rural poor
where field hands have been replaced by machines;
where pregnant women lack prenatal care,
and to the local clinic do not go
unless the "boss man" takes them—or unless
they've saved up enough hard-earned cash to pay.
Her people have no land to grow their food
while landowners are paid to rest their fields.
No welfare or relief checks come their way,
no unemployment checks or Social Security;
no governmental food program helps them.
Their sanitation does not get improved.
Their roads do not get paved, or wells, made safe
Some day there's no food in the house at all.

Her teenage sister Angela went North. Cousins say
she dropped school. They say she lives now
on the streets. Angela is being escorted
down a hall, through a leaden door the matron
      unlocks,
deep in bowels of City Jail,
where Time moves like a rodent in a trap,
flopping sometimes fast, sometimes slow.
Court session comes tomorrow.

She told the psychiatric doctor

enough times till he believed her:
no, no more will I try to kill myself.
So instead of committing her,
they brought her back to the bullpen.
But even so, they took away her bra
she had used, trying to strangle herself
by hanging herself under the bed in the cell.
And even so, even though
she swears to God Almighty in tears
this nineteen-year-old Lady Luck
carrying her first child,
she won't try to die no more—even so,
they won't trust her alone in a cell again.
They take her to the bullpen and close the door;
the bullpen with its turreted, aimed cameras;
with its combination steel fountain/toilet
plugged with paper towels and sandwiches.
Fifteen women are trying to recline
on a cement wallbench that sleeps twelve.
Fourteen, like her, are black and one is white.
It is 2:00 a.m. Of those awake,
two remember her and ask,
"Was it you, was screaming, they took out?"
and, looking at her belly
and marks around her neck,
figure why. "And why were you brought in?"
"Possession of a controlled substance ~ cocaine,"
she answers in a stammer, so softly.
And laughter then, from some, and stories:
how it went how some were caught. Stories:

cops they've slept with, where they go
to get their stuff, and prices, and stories.
Then there is a showing all around
of needle scars and bruises,
some rolling up sleeves and pants legs,
opening blouses to show each other
what puncture marks and inflamed veins
they carry on themselves
like stretchmarks or tattoos,
displaying them not proudly
or shamefully, either,
in self-condemnation,
but in exhibition
of explanation.
They are staring and nodding
at what they are seeing
when they look across the room
at each other.
"Yes," Angela tells the trembling group
she had tried to get a job and couldn't,
so to get welfare she got pregnant.
The matron brings in another prisoner
and bawls them all out for not sleeping.
Angela curls up on the floor in her fake fur jacket.
More than a lump in her throat rises in her,
more than a sob in her chest rises in her.
Something between a curse and a cry,
between a scream and a lullaby.
She tries to sleep. She tries to picture her baby,
but faces of the men keep coming to her mind,

especially the man in the big Cadillac
and the sailor she hopes is her baby's father.

There had not been enough light
for there even to be a shadow
in the dimly lit jail cell
before she tried to take her life.
She had folded her arms to make a cradle
and imagined him—her baby boy, brand new,
wrapped in a soft blanket; so tiny, sleeping.
Sitting on the steel bunk, her eyes tightly closed,
the song began to come from her again
as if it formed itself without her help:
"Little angel child close to mama's heart
you're a little man now
grow to be a soldier.
Trouble's all around us
need to make the world safe
grow to be a soldier
or a sailor like your daddy.
Little sweet one come to be my own
will you step into your daddy's shoes
so tall and brave in danger?
Baby darling breathing oh so soft
since your daddy's off to war
I'll buy a little sailor suit
so you can be a hero.
World's so full of trouble
need to make the world safe.
Got to fight the wars.

When your daddy's back in port
when I show you to him
there'll be lots of loving
'cause I'm giving him a little sailor man."

She felt the sharp, sudden pain she'd felt before
in her lower back, but in her belly, too.
She screamed. It was too soon to feel such things,
she knew.
Had she killed her unborn child with drugs?
No one answered when she screamed.
The darkened cell seemed suddenly so cold.
Would she die and wouldn't anybody care?
Is this what kind of world it really was?
She went to hang herself beneath the bunk.

When they checked her, after they took her out,
they told her they they thought she was okay.
Now lying on the sealed cement floor, shivering,
Angela goes to sleep picturing herself
pinching her baby's soft cheek
to help him latch to her nipple
as she had seen it done over and over again.
She feels sleep overtaking her "jitters,"
rest, taking hold like a grip, till she is numb,
even numb to the stone hardness beneath her,
until the cement couches her
like a gem in a stone.
She lies there like crumbling, brittle bones
of that little woman buried in Ethiopia

two hundred thousand years ago
who is the original mother
and common ancestor of all cultures.
After her lifetime of hunting and gathering
and suckling young at her breasts,
that mother sleeps under a stone
whose longings are sealed.

O Mitochondrial Mother of all
with genetics repeated repeated repeated
descendants like sands of Sahara unnumbered
O Matrix Mother of one human family
sleep now forever curled in a question mark
in the same position Angela sleeps
and the same way as her unborn child
curved like shoulders of a woman with a spear
peering into shadows in the bush
African mother of humankind
sleeps as if sleep is formed from a question
curved like a woman's wrist stirring with a spoon
curved like a hand covering a seed with soil
curved like the hunched back of an old woman
O so unquestioningly sleep, now sleep
She could be the black madonna of peace
holding out a dove, with her eyes as huge
as bronze medallions imprinted with her face;
the black madonna of all centuries,
who has been sculptured and enshrined like a goddess
all over the world, both in snow and in tropics,
bringing worshipers to a focal point

centered on black womanspirit,
black as soil rich in goodness,
the blackness of exquisite fertility,
earth supremely evoked to bountifulness.

Angela wakes, aching with back and leg cramps
and hunger pangs which make her cry.
She wakes, crying, her moan becomes a sobbing wail.
She wonders as she cries, does anyone anywhere
    hear?
Does anyone hear me crying, or my little baby
    crying?

Her cry is heard by the farmer in his field.
He cultivates his crop, bending to look back
over the rows of leafing plants
as he drives this tractor straight ahead.
He hears a cry, a hungry woman's cry,
and only knows to do as he is doing:
bringing a crop through from seed to harvest.
Angela cries out from what she dreamed in sleep:
how she stood in a supermarket aisle
with children and babes in her grocery cart,
all of them hungry including herself,
with food stamps to use for buying her food
for 83 ¢ per person per meal.
When she cries out in frustration
she is heard by the farmer in the field,
but between them looms an enormous wall
higher than well-stocked supermarket shelves.

a wailing wall jutting between hungry people
and the humanitarian heart of the farmer.
A wall made of paperboard, plastic and aluminum,
a wall made of tightly-bound bundles of money,
currency earmarked for advertising and handling,
for rail and truck transportation, for fuel,
electricity, repairs, refrigeration,
for property taxes, insurance, interest,
for rent, and before-tax-profits,
professional services, labor, accounting.
The wall between Angela and the food in the
    package
is made of steel, glass and brick
of corporate office buildings
where Angelas are never seen,
where farmers would be foreigners.
The wall made of the package that is access to food
bears messages boldly imprinted
saying "open" to some and "don't touch" to others
in bright colors and tantalizing designs,
words and instructions Angela can't read,
price tags she cannot afford to pay.
She is dwarfed by the towering supermarket shelves.
Her cry and the whimpering cry of her young
are drowned out by the Muzak played on the
    speakers.
Does anyone hear our cries? she wonders.
They are heard by the farmer in the field.
He hears their wailing in the wind
and turns his head, alert,

the same nerve touched
as when he hears a calf caught in a fence
or when his own child limps toward him
sobbing over a scraped knee or beesting.
The cry of urban poor who need food
tugs on his heart. Compassion
catches in his throat, then roars from him
as a deep groan thunderously echoing
from horizons east and west:
the heart of American heartland
responding to the cry of underfed people.

The farmer would feed the whole hungry world
if his will alone allowed.
He is as trapped in technicality
as Angela is trapped in poverty.
Their mutual lamentation is drowned out
by babbling of the Chicago Board of Trade
where, in the din on the floor
buyer, seller and speculator
harangue and wrangle.
The outcry of Angela and her children crying
and groan of the farmer's caring heart
are drowned out by the debate
over what the farmer should be paid
for his raw agricultural goods:
voices from the Board of Trade,
voices from acreages of desktops
of the Department of Agriculture.
Voices haggling over demand and scarcity,

yield, weather, growing conditions,
arguing over target prices and deficiency payments,
uttering economic indicators. Central
to all these considerations
is the speculator and his bank account,
not the survival of the hungry poor.

All the while this babble is going on,
Angela is crying into the cardboard wall
between herself and the packaged food.
She begins with moan, ends with wail.
Her cry is heard by the farmer in the field,
through that slick, slimy cellophane wall
stretched tightly over food like skin stretched over
    ribs,
she is heard, through the clear plastic seawall
drowning the farmer in cost for seeds,
for high-priced fertilizer and pesticides,
expensive machinery, costly repairs,
insurance, building maintenance, tools.

It's a cardboard wall thick as doormats by entrances
of Del Monte. Ralston-Purina, Cargill and
    Continental;
doormats thick as steaks held up to starving dogs
smilingly dangled in front of the dogs
who are then beaten, kicked and clubbed
when they leap to taste prosperity flaunted and
    denied.
Doormats, where walk the corporate giants

who process and distribute the food of this world,
where they wipe soil from their shoes.
Doormats like islands of extravagance
among the destitute;
thick doormats, thickening.
What shall the farmer be paid?
What shall the consumer pay for food?
The American dollar buys less
because the government overspends
on all things military and nuclear.
More of the consumer's paycheck is used
to buy a bag of groceries
due to the inflationary spending
on submarines, missiles,
artillery, bombers, land mines, bombs.
The farmer's costs are higher
The processor's costs are higher
The wholesaler's costs are higher
The transporter's costs are higher
The retailer's costs are higher
Higher because of the very high price
of the military slice.

The walls of the bread wrappers are blurry
as lenses of dimestore reading glasses
worn by limited income elderly.
They are blurry like goggles of perspiring welders
in the nuclear weapon assembly line
in Amarillo, Texas. They are clouded
like urine specimens of ill employees

in plutonium production in Richland, Washington.
The walls of the bread wrapper should be brought down
by the bitterness of people standing in line
in breadlines and souplines in the Soviet Union
and wherever American political obsession
with military power is imitated.

The walls of plastic milk containers
are bluish-gray like shattered glass
of television sets broken in rage.
The plastic is bluish-gray
like bruises on backs of children.
Milk containers are blue-gray
like hair of retired employees
of the nuclear weapon storage depot
in Waikele, Hawaii, who shop
to buy war toys for their grandchildren.
The plastic walls are bluish-gray
like air in the smoking lounge
at the Gaseous Diffusion Plant
in Paducah, Kentucky
where a worker of proud Greek descent
is reading a body-building magazine.
The walls should be brought down
by the misery of millions of refugees
and millions living in refugee camps,
many of whom are victims of war,
for all of them the prospect
of dying from starvation

being as much of a reality as daylight.

The walls of the meat wrapper are white
like powdered soap used to wash off
police fingerprinting ink.
They are white like foamy coats
of greyhound dogs racing as if
someone's life depended on it.
They are white like little bits
of cigarette wrapper left on stubs,
enough for a scrounger to have a smoke.
Butcher paper is white like milk
for schoolchildren of Aiken, South Carolina,
near the Savannah River Plant;
white like condoms used by grandsons
of Hiroshima survivors.
The walls of butcher paper should be brought down
by the agony of people in cultures
whose survival is so tenuous
that they rejoice at the birth
of a stillborn child.

The packing material dividing layers of oranges and
    apples
is soft like lottery tickets held tightly
in a sweaty palm; puffy like swollen eyelids
on the face of a battered woman.
Fruit carton dividers are soft like breasts
of female employees of Los Alamos Laboratory
during their mammograms.

They are soft like couches of therapists
counseling suicidal Viet Nam veterans.
They are soft like casket linings of children
who die from leukemia near test sites
for atomic weapons. The divisions
separating people from food
should be brought down by the hopelessness
of the millions starving in the very same countries
receiving military equipment and training
from the United States
to the tune of millions of dollars.

The walls of cans of vegetables and soup
are metal like grocery carts of street people.
They're metal like badges of New York City police
who evicted all homeless from Tompkins Square Park
one June morning. Soup and vegetable cans are metal
like spoons used in freebasing cocaine.
Their walls are metal like spoon collections
of naval officers' wives in Norfolk, Virginia.
They are metal like silver spoons
filled with ice cream
for the infant grandchildren of generals.
The walls should be brought down
by the grief of families and friends
of protestors killed by U.S.-made weapons
during peasant food riots in other countries.

The gaudy cardboard walls of cereal packages
are smooth like bald patches on scalps

of diabetic elderly women. They are smooth
like whisky bottles of unbathed men sleeping
in parks. Cereal boxes are smooth
like Christmas cards saying "Peace on Earth"
exchanged between Monsanto employees
in Miamisberg, Ohio.
They are smooth like photos of soldiers
still missing in action in Vietnam.
Bowling alleys are smooth like this
in Washington, D.C., where Pentagon employees
get one strike after another. Diners' Club cards
are this smooth, especially those belonging to
staff of the Lawrence Livermore Laboratories.
The walls should be brought down by the anger
of the 60 million rural landless of the world,
many of whom were ruined
by the distribution of U.S. farm commodities.

Frozen food packages are slimy like spittle
of old men with emphysema. They are slimy
like the stickiness of smashed cockroaches.
Frozen food packages' walls are slippery
and slimy, oozing like gangrenous infection
oozing from the bandaged legs
of faithful maids who in their age
are replaced by cleaning services.
The walls are slimy like toy bones
of the pedigreed dogs of Union Carbide executives
of Oak Ridge, Tennessee. They are slimy
like the sweaty hands of employees

driving through the gate of Rocky Flats Plant
in Golden, Colorado. The backs
of vomiting, anorexic daughters
of Sandia Laboratory's staff in Albuquerque
are wet and slimy like these walls.
The walls must be brought down
by the tragic moans of millions of peasants
whose sustenance has been overtaken
by multinational corporations
to raise rubber, cotton, sugar cane, tea,
cocoa and coffee as cash crops.

These walls must be brought down:
the lumpy walls of bags of potatoes.
They are lumpy like shopping bags
carried by homeless people.
They are lumpy like kimonos
worn by newborn addict babies.
Bulky and lumpy like body bags
containing dead soldiers.
Bulky like overweight security guards
at the neutron generator plant
in Clearwater, Florida. Lumpy
and bulky like protective bags
for the fur coats of members' wives
of the Department of Defense.
Will anguish bring down these walls?
In Mexico and elsewhere in the world,
millions eat less than 1500 calories
while their local food producers

grow and export large quantities of food.
Will their anguish bring down these walls?

And these walls: the clear glass walls
of baby food jars. They are clear
like car windows through which drug dealers
whisper their threats and make their deals.
They are clear like store windows
through which street people gaze upon
mannequins dressed to the hilt
and everything they'll never have.
The walls are clear glass like test tubes
filled with AIDS babies' blood.
They are clear like the glass
of telescopic sights. The walls
of baby food jars are clear glass
like goblets held up during toasts
by the head of the Department of Agriculture.
They resemble the pieces of windowglass
still being tweezed from the scalps
of survivors of the bombing of Hiroshima.
Will wretchedness bring down these walls?
African peasants and pastoralists starve
while agricultural aid
goes into irrigated systems of richer farmers.
Will their wretchedness bring down these walls?

The aluminum foil walls of candy kiss wrappers
are shiny like foil wrapped around
brown heroin, white cocaine, green marijuana.

They are shiny like foil packaging of pills
doled out to the mentally ill
standing in line at outpatient clinics.
Candy kiss wrappers are not unlike
the packaging of Valium and Xanax pills.
They are like what wraps Halcyon pills
given at night to nursing home residents.
The walls of candy kiss wrappers
are like the aluminum foil used by the homeless
to wrap around their bodies and their belongings
for weather protection. They are like
foil used for barbecuing food
for outdoor feasts of Bendix Corporation executives
in Kansas City, Missouri. They are like
wrappers of food used by astronauts
and food which will be stocked on space stations.
They are like foil wrappers of dog treats
rewarding the pets
of Star Wars designers.
The walls should be brought down
by the cry of hunger in America,
never before so piercing a cry,
so long and loud
as now.

Timothy Fay of the Route 3 Press, Anamosa, Iowa, designed and printed this edition of *End Hunger!* He printed 400 copies with a Miehle Vertical letterpress on Fox River Evergreen text. He and Eldon Meeks set the type in Intertype Kenntonian and handset Goudy Oldstyle. The Campbell-Logan Bindery, Inc., Minneapolis, bound the book.